Late Psalm

Late Psalm

BETSY SHOLL

The University of Wisconsin Press

The University of Wisconsin Press
1930 Monroe Street
Madison, Wisconsin 53711

www.wisc.edu/wisconsinpress/

3 Henrietta Street
London WC2E 8LU, England

Text design by Carol Sawyer of Rose Design

Library of Congress Cataloging-in-Publication Data
Sholl, Betsy.
Late psalm / Betsy Sholl.
    p. cm.
    ISBN 0-299-19890-1 (cloth : alk. paper)
    ISBN 0-299-19894-4 (pbk. : alk. paper)
I. Title.
PS3569.H574L38   2004
811'.54—dc22   2003022358

In memory of Beatrice Scott Keenan, 1903–1998
and Marjorie Hill Sholl, 1920–1999

as we go running round
this road, our pain is constantly renewed.
Did I say pain? Solace is what I mean!
—DANTE, *PURGATORIO*

Contents

Acknowledgments   xi

At the Public Market (*1*)   3

I

It Would Be Better If We Didn't Talk About It   7

Elegy with Postcard   9

Queen of the Night   11

Elegy with Trains   13

Half the Music   15

Leisure Village   18

Design in America   20

Back with the Quakers   22

Photographer   24

Homeless Encampment   26

In a Time of Drought   28

All Questions to Be Answered, *No*   30

Sweeney at Prayer   32

Vertical Melancholy   34

Louder   36

Little Elegy   38

Shore Walk with Monk   39

Solid Ground   41

BOARDWALK   43

EQUINOX   45

AFTER THAT   47

AT THE PUBLIC MARKET (*II*)   51

II

MESSENGERS FALLING TO OUR AID   55

HERE   57

BACKWASH   59

BASS LINE   61

TRANSITION   63

BOOK OF NUMBERS   65

THE BIRD SUIT   69

THE LIFE OF KEATS, SPARED BRIEFLY BY JOHN COLTRANE   71

EXCHANGE   73

TO WALT WHITMAN IN HEAVEN   75

READING   77

IMPEDIMENTS   78

SISTER   80

STRAY HORN   82

GOSPEL HOUR   84

MEDITATION, WITH OTHER VOICES   86

LATE PSALM   88

BECAUSE WE IMAGINE A JOURNEY   91

LAST BOAT   93

AT THE PUBLIC MARKET (*III*)   97

Acknowledgments

I would like to thank the editors of the following magazines in which versions of these poems first appeared:

Alaska Quarterly Review: "Book of Numbers"

Animus: "Homeless Encampment"

The Beloit Poetry Journal: "Elegy with Trains," "At the Public Market (i)"

Brilliant Corners: "Shore Walk with Monk," "The Life of Keats, Spared Briefly by John Coltrane," "Equinox," *"Transition"*

Crab Orchard Review: "To Walt Whitman in Heaven," "Impediments," "In a Time of Drought," "After That"

Drexel Online Journal: "Photographer," "It Would Be Better If We Didn't Talk About It"

Field: "Backwash," "Because We Imagine a Journey," "The Bird Suit," "Sweeney at Prayer," "Vertical Melancholy," "Back with the Quakers"

5AM: "Little Elegy," "Leisure Village"

The Green Mountains Review: "Design in America," "Solid Ground"

The Journal: "Exchange"

Kenyon Review: "Late Psalm"

The Maine Times: "Boardwalk " (under the title "Old Orchard Beach")

The Massachusetts Review: "Half the Music"

The Nebraska Review: "Last Boat"

Poetry Miscellany: "At the Public Market (iii)"

Prairie Schooner: "Queen of the Night," "Elegy with Postcard," "Messengers Falling to Our Aid"

Rivendell: "Bass Line," "Here"

Shenandoah: "Gospel Hour"

Sou'wester: "Louder," "Meditation, with Other Voices"

Third Coast: "Sister," "Stray Horn"

"Half the Music," "Queen of the Night," and "Late Psalm" were reprinted in *Poets of the New Century*, edited by Roger Weingarten and Richard Higgerson.

"Late Psalm" was reprinted in *A Cappella: Mennonite Voices in Poetry*, edited by Ann Hostetler.

"Here" was reprinted in *The Maine Poets*, edited by Wesley McNair.

"Backwash," "Shore Walk with Monk," "Half the Music," "The Life of Keats, Spared Briefly by John Coltrane," "Gospel Hour," "Stray Horn," "Queen of the Night," and "*Transition*" appeared in a limited edition chapbook from Oyster River Press.

Heartfelt thanks to the many people who read this manuscript: Susan Aizenberg, Ted Deppe, Nancy Eimers, Lynn Emanuel, Lee Hope, David Jauss, Natasha Saje, Jody Stewart, Leslie Ullman, Tony Whedon, David Wojahn, Baron Wormser, Carolyne Wright, the Portland poetry group. Special thanks to Ron Wallace. And, always, to Doug Sholl.

Late Psalm

At the Public Market (*1*)

Abandon all hope, reads the hand-scrawled sign
propped beside the lobster tank—some joker
brooding on its murky doom, which looks

more like the world unformed and void,
stirred by a mind feeling that sluggish urge
to make itself known, a mind struggling

into form, water to gel, to claw and tail,
oozing its way out of slime, stumbling
among bottom feeders, grovelers, creeps

all bunched up, feelers adither
over their future's watery inferno.
How innocent Dante seems at first—

trembling and clutching at Virgil his guide,
as if he hadn't constructed that bucket
of dry ice himself, and personally

tossed each specimen in. Such a din
of marketing all around, it's easy
to be wilted by guilt, or to rage at

whoever made this place. But to watch
how lobsters madly scramble, you have to
bend close, look through your own shadow

into the tank's dim algae light,
where a few black beads fiercely eye back—
grabbers and pinchers clawing their way

to the top of some little heap.
And for what? I suddenly have to ask,
trembling, here, in the middle of my life.

I

It Would Be Better If We Didn't Talk About It

What do I know of this extravagant
spendthrift green, oblivious to the future,

trying to talk the being of Being with me
in foreign signs, gesturing with multiple limbs?

Early summer trees know secrets
they keep waving through the window,

as if I could understand someone
mouthing words across an enormous field.

But I learned summer in childhood
from a feverish mystery simply called "glands."

Nothing to read but old religious books
with blissed-out pilgrims dressed in rags.

Whole weeks that summer they trudged
through blizzards, from shrine to shrine,

content with dried bread, with dogs snarling
at their heels, the physical world just so much

flare and delusion. All the same to them,
mouths empty or full of bright ivory,

a hot musty bed or the beach's dazzle.
But I was young then, just beginning to learn

about fever, how all our lives we burn
for something that trembles just out of reach.

It would be better if we didn't talk
about it, these green leaves flickering,

little parables, trying to explain
what it takes to break wood into blossom.

Elegy with Postcard

for Shirley Roses

A cloudless day, one forsythia bud
just unfolding its first flute note of spring,
and I'm lingering in autumn rains,
in a Japanese print sent by a friend

fifteen years ago—its old pilgrim
with clogs and a walking stick still making
his difficult way against thick slashes
of rain, as if their purpose were to stab,

to slow him down so he feels every pelt
and sting of that stormy crossing, cold
garments slapping his flesh. For years
I've tried to guess what the characters say

there, in the upper right corner: *Friend,*
cold rain and howling winds slow me, but thoughts
of you pull me on. Or: Friend, what shitty times—
to be exiled in late autumn. Friend,

this is the third spring without you. Longer still
since that grim disease entered your lungs.
All the things you loved—jazz, pungent coffee,
foreign films with their sideshow grotesques,

meandering Fellini-esque parades
of grief and desire—each bears a figment
of you, your scent, voice, your wit flickering . . .
And the way, as everything else darkened,

your irony grew almost benign
until one day you said, *Even for this
I am grateful*—it's as if you stumbled on
the translation of that lone pilgrim's

mysterious thoughts. We were walking
through noon mist and crowded streets. Mid-block
you gripped my arm to rest, then started again,
barely lifting your feet, but still intent

on our last lunch in that tiny storefront
Korean restaurant, whose food by then
you could only smell and prod with chopsticks
across the plate's dark blue mountain pass.

QUEEN OF THE NIGHT

FOR RUTH WELTING

They're not gone yet, those notes she lifts
from deep inside, like a quarterback
she says, lofting up and out, not knowing
if they'll be caught or spin down off orbit
and slip from the receiver's hands. Last week
they soared across the opera's stadium

so everyone received the pass. *Brava! Brava!*—
five full minutes before they let her go.
Next day, she walked up to the gate, got bumped
flight after flight, as if from elation, she says—
as if it's a law: one day the Met, the next
you can't get out of bed. There's the time she rose

from the basement on a tiny platform—
no rails, stagehands had to stuff her skirts—
but something snagged on the wobbly ascent
into smoke and lights, so just as her aria
climbed to its heights her skirts came undone.
Comic version, same rule: whatever rises, falls.

Sometimes, though, it seems to go another way:
that voice arriving uninvited to both her sister
and herself, lifting them out of such a lowdown
childhood, for years those bad times still bubbled
and steamed underneath any stage they were on,
like the opera's cave of death, its dry ice

and writhing souls backlit on a gauzy veil.
Once she blew that voice off in smoke rings and slurs,
didn't ask for it back, though it came, deepened
into parts she'd been too high for: the Queen's
daughter, who pleads to her lover's back—
pure *sehnsucht*, "longing beyond longing,"

the part her sister sang, whose own stupendous voice
was choked off in a husband's seething rage—
no one there to hear the last cries crushed
in that throat. *Sehnsucht*. Over tea,
she closes her eyes, and that aria wells up
then trails off to such thin decibels,

such quiet notes they could sift through loam
and stir the dead—if longing didn't dissolve
before it got to bone, if motion didn't
involve both rise and fall, sack and Hail Mary,
the Met's bright cheers, then next morning's lone soul
at the gate, ordinary voice seeking flight.

Elegy with Trains

My friend would tell the story of those two men
who don't know where the train is going,
so after it stops at a depot in that sham
of a real journey, they run to climb back on
the boxcars gathering speed, heading

for Bergen-Belsen. Hard to talk after that.
Though once pushing strollers we respun the facts,
made vodka-numbed Nazis chuckle *lucky
bastards* and shrug as the engine chugs on,
so the two dapper young men race

then gasp, slumping down on the tracks
at the start of their spared lives. That's where
it always broke down, my friend's head full
of ghetto stats, the true story of trains—
Spared? I can still see her stop and glare,

You call that spared? Across different cities
and twenty years our conversation ran: *Scratch
a gentile deep enough, and you get a Nazi . . .
Who can say they wouldn't collaborate . . .*
Then this turned up in her parents' safe

deposit box: a photo marked *Poland*—
grandparents she thought had died in a trench
they dug themselves at bayonet point,
but here they are grinning while sunlight
beams on a sleek, finned sedan—hidden

all these years, as if it had been heresy
to her folks that someone survived, happy
to drive away from those trains in such
a big fishy car. Her folks, who lived through
the war in Brooklyn, as if in shame,

vowing never to find life sweet again,
never to wait underground without
staring down the track's long perspective
into that vanishing point of bitter graves.
I was suicidal, my friend said,

until I got cancer. We were walking
a steep hill, ice cream cones in our hands,
stopping every few yards to rest,
her unshaded eyes staring at rose vines,
jet trails, late sun on brick—drinking them in.

That was the last time we met, so I don't
have to picture her dying on the year's
longest night, struggling for breath, alone
in her apartment, only those grandparents
framed beside her: my friend, whose silver loops

now hang from my ears, whose two earnest men
won't stop racing after that train. I don't
have to picture it slowing down, or the look—
we could never decide on the look—
in the guards' eyes, when they put out their hands.

HALF THE MUSIC

What's that noise? my stepfather asks,
hearing all the way from Florida the falling racks
of cassette tapes the plumber knocks off the wall.
What's that racket? he repeats, quick relief
from his sad story of how many times
my mother has fallen this week, how little she eats.

It's just the new hot water heater
getting wrestled from kitchen to cellar,
and half the music of my life crashing
to the floor, plastic cases split, lids snapped off
and skittering across the tile, as sax,
blues harp, piano unravel, toss and turn—

like my stepfather last night, waking
to phone-fright and a sweltering apartment,
air conditioner shot. Fear-soaked, he reached
for the receiver, expecting the night nurse,
but it was just some drunk dialing random
from God knows where, *Hey, man, howya doin?*—

which almost could be God, if the words
weren't slurred, if the voice gave a shit
how scary it was, that shrill in the night
making an old man think whatever he's
tethered to just broke. He's got grief
clogged in his throat, talking these blues,

and others too—how his legs ache,
all shaky, betraying the brain's commands.
We're on the fritz, he says, meaning my frail
mother with her panic and tears, her broken
words like birds on a wire that scatter
and rebunch, one note hopping to the end

of the line, so the song's frayed, always
changing, and my mother weeps that she can't
keep it straight, weeps like someone with no tongue,
who can't say what she knows, though we strain
to grasp like woodsmen chasing
some mythical bird song into thick forests,

seduced by its tenuous trill, haunting
and almost clear, till we're lost in a craze
of branches, no path, no light overhead—
except my stepfather's ever-ready
yellow pad, his new list: three end-of-life
scenarios he clears his throat and reads now,

though I try not to hear how the tree
I've lived in all my life could crash,
ripping out a big patch of ground; or, *two*,
could remain standing but turn stark
and barren from lightning's quick stroke;
or, *three*—but I have to say stop, stop,

it's too sad, this sparrow, her music spilled,
the tissues and cups on her bedside stand
she fumbles for and knocks on the floor,
then falls trying to reach. Nothing to do
but wail out our sorrow, our phones hot
from the breaths dissolving between us,

and I can't talk about the little bird
I found on the sidewalk this morning,
sparrow-like, with brown flecks on its wings
and a bright yellow belly, I picked up
and held, its death in my hands, and my heart
flying full speed as if straight at plate glass.

Leisure Village

To sleep through this pack of blackbirds
and their constant quarrels, the residents
here must be deaf. How disconcerting

to be roused at dawn, the guest room eaves
a scene of high drama, and you, yawning
on the balcony, irrelevant to the plot.

Though what else is such a place about,
if not these wings, folks getting used to
bit parts? Now some walk-ons:

one almost limber, others playing their roles
so well you can feel the stiff knee, fused spine,
the grumble in your own mind, as husband

and wife lumber five feet apart. That is,
if you're a daughter just come to visit,
in mid-life herself. But if you're a blackbird,

what are these to you, such awkward walkers,
these flightless non-hoppers, mincing along
as if each shadow could be the top stair

about to pitch them into a cellar?
That is, if you notice them at all,
having a reputation to defend, a tree,

a worm garden, some pesky flitting thing
to shoo away from your squabbling nest.
And when you're old, when you're ready to die?

But that's a Masonic secret you never
divulge, not to these decrepit grounders
with their loud mouths and bad tempers.

If they notice at all, let them watch you
enter a glinting palm, and not come out. Let them,
with their clouded eyes, stand there and gawk.

DESIGN IN AMERICA

Behind the art museum, the sky slips
its frame, unraveling in random clouds,
subject indeterminate, though down the block
an old man dressed in sandwich boards
shouts *repent,* convinced the theme is ruin,

and it's his job as people pass to hiss:
Behind your pretty face—worms!
Behind your fancy car—flames!
But when he pistol-points at me: *Your soul's*
a hollow brick—it's as if I knew

all along when I set out this morning
in a new dress to view what the art
museum says changed the future
of design in America, some nut
would shake a crooked finger, and I'd start

to crumble: one minute—content, looking
at giant Marilyns, all flat and broken up
into dot matrix, the next—out on the sidewalk's
gritty slabs, being told that below these rocks
other rocks bubble and steam in earth's black pot.

And if this scrawny guy, slathered with
bumper stickers about doom's invisible curtains
ready to drop, is right? Well, the ex-con
on his stool outside the coffee shop just shakes
his head and keeps on making tin foil wolves,

aluminum horses, hand-crimped trees
filled with Reynolds Wrap birds, and like a god
who can't bear to let one sparrow drop—
what he messes up he twists into leaves,
into little wads of cocoon, slightly cracked.

BACK WITH THE QUAKERS

You think you can handle these things:
sunlight glinting off a red Jaguar
honking at the old woman who has snagged

her shopping cart on a snow rut,
or the swaggering three-piece suit who steps
outside the bank, earless to the mossy voice

at his feet asking for spare change,
but then the crunch of something, nothing really,
under your shoe—a dirty comb, a pen cap—

completely undoes you, and it's too much,
too much, being balanced, considering
the complexity of all sides in one

syntactically correct sentence.
All the driver has to say is, "Move it,
Lady," and you're back with the Quakers

who trained you to lie still and limp in the street.
Three days they stepped on your hair,
ground cigarettes half an inch from your nose,

while you lay there, trying to be against
violence, your fists tight as grenades
and a payload of curses between your teeth,

O woman, with a mind Picasso
could have painted, giving you many cheeks,
each one turned a different way.

PHOTOGRAPHER

AUGUST SANDER, 1876–1964

Notary, Butcher, Repossessor:
  his ambition—to collect them all,
    to catalogue the age. But *Writer*,
Varnisher, Village Band—the types divide,
  individuate. So, he takes more:
    City Children, warily eyeing him,
Widower with Sons, slumped in grief.
  He believes we can see things as they are,
    the whole flux, "favorable to us or not."
Then a wind blows through the streets of Cologne,
  across the clothesline strung on his roof,
    knocking a print loose, the photograph
fluttering down into a citizen's hand,
  confiscator's fist. "This isn't truth,"
    the Nazis sneer—*Transvestites* on pages
facing *Aryan Youth*, so when the book's closed
  they kiss. Still, he insists: *Cretin, Tramps,*
    Dwarves—things as they are, not the myth.
After wind, come secret police, bombs.
  Then war's end, and fire set by looters
    finally burns the plates he's buried,
as if an age could categorically refuse
  to let itself be known, disdaining
    our glance, like these two *Bohemians*,
so fixed on each other they seem to say
  we can't possibly know what they see,
    or this *Unemployed* man, hat in hand

on the empty street, head shaved—
   has his hair been sold, spent?
      Or these: *Circus People*, lounging
beside their caravan, clustered around
   an old Victrola—record on, needle down—
      who stare as if they're trying to hear
how the tinny song thins as it passes
   through the lowered gaze of a woman
      leaning at the door, as it grazes
the black man's braided suit, presses
   against his wary eye, fixed—now
      that no one else is left—on us.

Homeless Encampment

As if a creature had flown all night
through layers of firmament with a word
or curse, a creature resting a little first—

until he sits up and slowly morphs
into a young man on the courthouse lawn
under a pile of—not wings—but quilts

with appliquéd petals radiating
from faded cores, a young man on a bed
of grass tufted with cigarette butts, fringed

with placards protesting the city's lack
of shelter. And has the music
from this idling car picked up his dream

amped into the singer's angry rasp,
then the electric guitar smashing
what's left of the song like an ax

wracking the whole damn thing to ruin,
to rain-blistered wood, torn strings, racket
of grackles nesting in the wreck . . . ?

That must be what our city planners fear,
the whole place on bad brakes skidding
toward *cosmic crash*, apocalypse in shrill

feedback. Though now the taut pitch snaps,
and melody resumes, as if to croon,
There's more to the story, always more.

But first, the protesters will have to endure
a week of storms, their encampment drenched,
children ponchoed in plastic bags, shivering

under tarps weighed down with pools of rain
that suddenly let loose—all that,
before those of us passing by will stop

and read the signs disintegrating
into inky blurs, will look and feel our own hair
running in cold rivulets down our backs.

In a Time of Drought

Are there languages in this world with forty different names
for the ways rain falls? Could tongues stiffened by English, used to *drizzle*
and *mist*, ever loosen enough to learn liquid vowels and consonantal
  clatter?
Are there names for rain that stays in the clouds like a sullen adolescent,
and garrulous rain yakking all the way down? Rain heavy as sheet metal,

darning needle rain, rain berries on twigs, rain without a country to
  fall on—
my young friend is a husband without a wife, having married by proxy
his girlfriend, who still lives in their native land where rain surges in
on dark clouds each afternoon, crashes down like buckets
dumped on the jungle, then rises again in green steamy veils. There,

our tight-roofed embassy won't give visas to anyone intimate
with downpours: no deluging immigrant rain washing out coastlines
as citizens board up their windows, no rain rushing the drains, mobbing
  streets.
But what if thunder means more than we think, and lightning's electric
  cursor
will someday write in the sky the questions we fear: Citizens,

were you plenteous as rain, did you pour down on the needy,
run through the streets in torrents like mercy, did you fall on thatch
and plastic tarp, were you slow and easy entering drought-hard ground,
or did you drop your relief and roar off? Rain with its delicate beaded
  curtains,
with its scepters of light, acid rain, seed rain, rain runnels and scum—

it isn't this that is ruining my friend's dream of balloons at the airport,
a crowd cheering as his bride steps down the ramp, sun in her wake,
and outside, watery diamonds shining on wires and trees. American rain?
African rain? Rain moving across the oceans between, falling
and rising again—is it falling now on the documents a young woman

clutches to her body for shelter as she waits in line outside the embassy
with its iron gates and drenching overhangs, its official indelible stamps
the rain can't smudge? Rain without borders, needing no permission
  to fall:
fall now on the eyes of the civil servants, dampen their stiff resolve,
let them see this woman dripping from her eyebrows and braided hair,

holding her rain-dimpled papers, for the third time standing before them
requesting permission. Let them know how it feels to kiss a young man
under wide tropical leaves, and laugh when they tip like saucers
dousing you, as you pledge your steady and intermittent, your stormy
and soft, your scattered and lavish, bank-breaking rain.

All Questions to Be Answered, *No*

I thought of snow, but it was still summer.
  I pictured my friend doing the mashed potato
    to James Brown in her living room, but she
was in bed wincing when she turned, bald,
  testy with death. Is laughter gone forever?
    Sometimes I just like saying it: *No.*
Will we ever stop longing to feel
  feathers spread out from our arms, a tail
    at our waists, little twiggy feet—and blue,
can we please be blue? Can we give up
  words and just scat, eat, fuss a little,
    soar and sleep? Lord of the scabrous,
Lord of street theater and widowers,
  of the timorous and blustering, are we
    allowed to be tired, to pull down the shades,
to feel grateful for who we are—not like
  the pudgy child in the supermarket
    fingering cookies, the skinny mother
who yanked him away, then flicked me off
  with her eyes? Lord of my friend reading
    mysteries all night when the pain wakes her,
Lord of women who do amazing things
  with hair: huge fountains, wedding cakes of hair—
    I see their clients every Friday on the bus.
Lord of the bus, of the standing and seated,
  the tax collector longing to weep
    in his rented car—will we ever be done

with grieving, with little boys singing
　　to their lunch boxes, brittle mothers
　　　with chemical hair? Sweet Lord of hair,
beaded curtains and narrow fringes—the girl
　　on the bus telling her friend, "I know a kid
　　　grows marijuana in his hair"—thick falls
and little sprouts, conks, tonsures, wigs
　　the wind can't dishevel, and underneath,
　　　underneath—will we ever be done?

SWEENEY AT PRAYER

he was filled with a restless tottering unquiet . . . from the curse
of Ronan bird-quick in craze and madness from the battle.
                    —FLANN O'BRIEN, *At Swim Two Birds*

Why Sweeney haunts me while I wait outside
the ICU has something to do with wind-blown
pigeons on the sill, the family gathered
in one house, filling every bed, and snow
falling for days, blustery winds, sleet on glass:

Sweeney, who couldn't keep his battles
to himself, or wait for the appointed time,
but had to spear-chuck the priest's cleric,
till din of battle or Father Ronan's curse
drove him to the woods in skittish fright,

all stumble and thrash, lurching into liftoff,
huffing himself up like a lumpy dove.
Down here, the bypass surgeon tells the truth
when he says he'll do some damage.
Face blackened, body pierced with tubes,

her monitors pulse, but no mother's there,
she's flown off, roosting somewhere in the room,
and no one knows how soon she'll come back,
if she's strong enough to press against
whatever rubs out kings and aging women,

those nettles within and without, divided
loyalties, mental unmoorings. Better is it

to be mad, perched in scruffy boughs
griping about the cold or some thorny bed,
all groan and grief?—though still, in song after song,

loving grouse, gull, stag cry, and every kind
of tree, except the human family's.
In her room all we do is coo, smooth pillows,
hover helpless against this violent cure.
Did they operate with bats and chains?

She's broken enough, impossible to lure
back from her woods. Rub forehead or hand,
and her lids flutter, but off she flits,
refusing to land, as if baited by Sweeney,
leap after leap, till they're so far out

on a limb, it buckles and chucks them
to the ground, giving what reason didn't.
Reason, with its monitors and tubes.
There are prayers it's a terror to say,
it's snow hurl, wind bite, ice dam on roof,

plaster and sky howling down, as if you
had begged: *make my mistakes worse*,
prayers you say bent over with your face
in your hands, feeling the cheekbones, knuckles
and knees you will one day become,

lice-ridden prayers, nothing to do with
what you wanted, with *sorry* or *please*—
they clabber the mouth with nettles,
with longing and muck, hurling you
heart-sore and hoarse into the flimsiest trees.

VERTICAL MELANCHOLY

Poor moth-eaten lawn, weedy and pissed on,
poor maple trees, dry and brittle in June.
I came out to read de Andrade
tell himself *Carlos, keep calm, love is what
you're seeing now* . . . And maybe I dozed,

that's why in just four stanzas the sky's grown
heavy as rumpled bed sheets. Now a creak,
casket-like, from a scary movie,
or a sign swinging on one rusty hinge
in a storm. Birds content with bare branch

markings on their backs. That creak again—*saints
crossing themselves, vertical, melancholy?*
Or just these two slender trunks rubbing
each other? Desperate, undomesticated
tree-love, here in my parched yard

where the clothesline has squealed on its pulleys
all spring, and my friend will never again sit,
asking, "Why don't you throw out that wreath?"
still hanging on the fence, hardly more brown
than the leaves—color of choking, her voice

trying to clear itself, that shallow cough.
And her husband can do nothing now,
her teenage daughter can't find a book
long enough, deep enough to hide in.
And now the first raindrops magnify the words,

Love in the dark, no, love in the daylight,
is always sad. Because the last hinge
wears thin, words blur, puckered by rain?
What are words, anyway? Let rain
with its pure invisible ink write this

letter to the trees, to the men and women
in their motels, lying in one another's arms—
today a kiss, tomorrow no kiss . . . Let rain
fall on the person writing these words
who for once doesn't care what she'll do

with the heavy weight of afternoon
falling like flowers dropped on her friend.
It's useless to resist . . . Let rain ask all the bereft:
Could even this be love, love in the dark,
no, in the daylight, what is pouring now?

LOUDER

The morning is white with mist
swirling off hay bales, pouring
from the nostrils of cows, mist
coating the car—wide acres
of mist, and hidden within
a convention of skeptics,
these rude crows with loudspeakers
announcing that everything's
a husk. Louder than the steam
kettle whistling next-door,
louder than the shifting gears
of a coal truck speeding up
on the down grade, milkweed puffs
rising in its wake—this dark
infestation of voices
saying *husk* to whatever
objection I make. *Husk*—these
late roadside purple asters,
stray dog nosing among them,
my son waiting for the bus,
its gears barely audible
on the next hill over this
raucous raving. The future?
Don't make them laugh—it's paper
before the wind's match, dry lips
slipping from a boy's soft cheek
as he runs to catch the bus,

the fog now a long tongue stretched
across the valley. The sun
not yet over the mountain,
but *husk* all the same, about
to enflame this mown field, gleam
on its dried stalks, on these grim
cynics, making the dark chaff
of their wings iridescent.

LITTLE ELEGY

oh how he loved his cup
and now he's dirt
under the pine trees
                    —LI PO

A moment of silence at Soup Kitchen
for our saint of the quick grip, faking
a side stitch to hide the bottle under his coat,

for his taped shoes and worm-eaten watch cap,
that clarifying fish pier scent, raw-grained
and terrifying smell of the skids,

how little it takes to wake up over a grate,
half-dissolved in shadow and mist—
half-dissolved, but still blissed out, bantering

with buddies, flailing on icy streets,
then catching hold of a lamppost and nodding
to it, to the sky, the glittery walk,

to a passing taillight, an old belief,
foolish or fearless, that everything's sacred,
and now he's gone.

Shore Walk with Monk

Whoever lived here is gone, but a slick
staircase remains in the broken shell,
damaged just enough to suggest secret
recesses spiraled inside where *something*
slid down to poke out its head,

and when a threat appeared, scurried
or oozed back along those pearly halls.
Someone stood catatonic when shaken down
by cops, but when he felt safe on the bandstand
he'd step out and dance, flap his elbows

like nubby wings, then back to the keyboard
to pick up his place, foot kicking
the piano's invisible flywheel.
Those were the years everyone changed shape,
painters squinted, poked their heads outside the frame.

Why have frames at all—or canvas, or paint?
And why not play the least expected note
so the music's a double exposure,
what's there and what isn't superimposed,
a musical house all fretwork and jut,

as if any minute the whole structure
might topple. But a house, once you've entered,
nothing four-square will do. You want those
crooked doors, those circular steps ending
in pure misterioso, you need

those rooms suspended over a bay
where sunlight keeps changing tempo and key—
or so I was thinking when my tape started
to chirp like a hip calliope,
and I took it out to see if I could rewind,

finger holding one reel, pencil turning
the other, like one of his visitors
fidgeting while Monk sits wordless for hours
or grinds his teeth. Funny, how he gets me out
of my own head's maze, its slippery hall of mirrors,

when he could go so far inside his own,
nothing moved but his eyes. Or he'd spend days
in constant motion, pacing and spinning
till the turbulence inside finally found
a room with a bed and laid itself down.

Weeks it could take to stumble back out—
which might explain all the doors and tilted
balconies in his musical house,
Magritte windows with their starry skies
painted on glass, while a perilous void

expanded inside. I'm off the beach,
beside my car by now, unraveling
a Mobius strip of Monk, Monk billowing
over dune grass and rocks, ringing the car's
antenna, Monk in hundreds of tiny

accordion pleats I couldn't undo
no matter how I try, all spiraling out
of their plastic shell, catching the light, pouring
a kind of broken music the maker's
done with, just slipped out of and left behind.

SOLID GROUND

Hurricane tide, a sudden drop—
  an inexplicable urge to draw closer,
    one step at a time onto slippery rocks,

and even though you wake from the craziness
  of one wave thrashing another,
    even though you don't get tumbled

till your stare turns pearl-blank and smooth,
  you learn that immersion fills the lungs
    with a deadly emulsion,

turns a girl into a negative
  overexposed, a child who saw too much
    like the cabin boy in *Moby Dick*,

jangled by all that sea, nothing but width
  and depth and—
                 nothing in all directions . . .

      After that you'll stand on shore watching
        the satiny wobble of sea, just foam
      at your feet. Over and over you'll read

      how high on the Pequod's mast a dreamy
        Platonist gazes at the vast dazzle,
      and discontent with such a little drift

of half-knowing, leans out farther and farther.
  On deck, sailors check harpoons, make lines
ready for a sighting of fluke or spout.

There—in the distance, something flickers.
  Ahab smolders, forging himself sharp
and hard in that foundry of a heart.

And who hasn't felt him inside,
  his one ivory leg's insistent *I*
wanting to destroy whatever wounds?

But also inside, a depth-crazed stammering girl
  whose life flashed before her jangled eyes.
    She wants only to sing: how she fell through

the sea's shifting mirrors, its waves
  of distortion, slid down green chutes onto
    watery conveyors, rumbled through beaters,

spinners and drums to come out unconscious
  but alive on the tawny rain-pocked beach.
    Rust-colored storm fence blown to a slant,

black wire slung across a textured sky—
  Even now, when I pray for solid ground,
    this is what I see. And the rest

is mystery, shimmery ladders of light,
  blizzards of froth, sun spot, sea flume,
    green terror and luminous jewel.

Boardwalk

I was sitting there thinking, this is how
the mystics argue: One cries like a nut,

"Listen to me, I'm crazy." Another shouts,
"For the sake of God, the Real, gamble

yourselves away." They'd say our hands,
this table, these beer mugs are nothing.

And what we buy in stores, insure, put on
résumés? Counterfeit, cheap tricks, kitsch,

amusement rides that tilt and whirl
along the water's edge, then come to a stop—

mere distraction from the sea itself,
in which we are so small and gelatinous

there's no telling where it ends and we begin—
or do *we* end where *it* begins?

Easy to panic, my friend, order another round,
say everything's rigged. But what if there's

really nothing to fear, if every time
we breathe out, what rushes in is crazily

in love with us, its one continuous body
of air oblivious to boundaries?

Neon, juke music, games of skill and chance,
high rolling waves, spray rising off the curl—

how silly wet suits and nose plugs seem
when standing here we're already immersed.

EQUINOX

Jasmine, oleander, not yet magnolia—
  March in Florida, close to the equinox.
    Herons and egrets waded in the shallows,
      in the rest home lagoon, dipping for fish,
  little flittering wishes and regrets.

Above the bench where my stepfather dozed
  two crows perched on streetlights screeched back and forth,
    their harsh ecstasies etching every petal
      and leaf in sight. Like dueling saxophones
  their music reached toward hearing-aid shrill,

the radio dial's far end where high-pitched
  static comes in, leached from the stars, if it's true
    everything sings. Then this would be the world
      slowing down, creaky joints, squealing brakes.
On and on they went, such strident airs

I hardly knew there was something else too,
  a fluting—no, flowering in a tree, a bird
    whose name I asked people who'd cup their ears,
      but still couldn't hear. And now it's gone,
  that sense of leafy sweetness in the shadows

where a song sprouted from the inner boughs
  and lingered a long time, not telling its name,
    why it hid in its green tent. I still ache to recall
      that quick little heart bent on making
a tune to savor everything it hears

near equinox, equal night and day, edge
   between gain and loss, as if the world had gears
      stiff at first, ratcheting us up, then—pause,
         a brief stasis before the earth tips
   toward or away from light, plummeting some.

Some? the crows scoffed, while the hidden bird
   just fluted higher, as if climb and plunge
      can't be divided, shadow and light,
         that tiny soul pent up in its tender body,
   aching, but not for words, no, not words.

Its song was wordlessly rent from the tree
   in petals descending like scent teasing me
      into wanting to be its wanting, just
         wanting to be outside that tree
   in leafy shade like someone waiting in line.

AFTER THAT

In Lakewood, New Jersey, they'd rock all day
on the porch of the old Jewish hotel—women
sputtering like those newsreels of Europe,
where they must have trudged through snow
in battered boots with newspaper socks,
looking for streets that no longer existed.

Back and forth they'd rock, muttering like pigeons,
old women who rolled their stockings just
to the knees as if that was dressing enough.
And they'd huff themselves out of their chairs
as if rising even a little was more than too much.
All through childhood's eyeglasses and cavities,

through first pumps with skinny five inch heels
and pointy toes, I couldn't walk fast enough
past that chorus of mourners lined up,
davening in wicker chairs, unstoppable clocks,
cradles endlessly rocking the world's woes,
dividing who saw from who shut their blue eyes.

I thought they only stopped the heavy creak
of their grief when I walked past. New shoes
dyed to match a prom gown, new lipstick, blush—
I'd swear they looked and scoffed. But maybe
they didn't notice me at all. Maybe
they were just grinding the past down

to one coarse meal of bone. Still, I can't
enter a store without hearing their voices—
so much vinegar even God would shudder,
would rummage through bins, wanting
to give them something, anything at all,
those fierce widows rocking forever

on the guest house porch, refusing to enter,
refusing to leave, having outlasted whole cities.
What would you ask for after that—
Some bright pleasure, a new truth?
Loden green pumps with stiletto heels?
That the world end, that the world continue?

At the Public Market (*II*)

The flesh of swordfish swirls like wood grain
around a knot, and the tuna's a dark rose,
its petals packed tight beside the bright
fine-grooved salmon making raw seem sweet:

such a beautiful display of how we eat
and are eaten. The crabs, oysters, mussels,
big and bigger shrimp in their gray shrink-wrap—
imagine not being able to eat,

having to repeat the rounds of these stalls
stunned like the gluttons on Terrace Six, who look
but can't touch as hunger crawls through muscle
and mind. Imagine the millionth time passing

bins piled with scallops like the jellied whites
of eyes collected by a mad despot.
And bass on ice, tiered rows of snapper,
gold racing stripes lined up with such care

each bright red unblinking bull's-eye is clear—
a good kind of grief Dante manages to say,
reading on each passing face shrunk down
to skull the word *Omo* (man), as if life

is a hunger we shouldn't rush to quell,
as if we shouldn't even want to dull
our appetite's relentless drive
till it arrives at what can't be consumed.

II

MESSENGERS FALLING TO OUR AID

Sometimes everything dazzles—broken glass
on the river bank, rain dimpling the sand.
But aren't there days you'd gladly slip like a dime

through the silver slats of the boardwalk
and dissolve in the pastel froth the tide swirls?
That's why, when noonlight suddenly obliterates

the surface of every leaf, we need a voice to linger
in our minds, whispering *let go*, or *go on*,
need lip-shaped window smudges where something

invisible has kissed us. Wind turning our clothes
inside out, coffee making a stranger's breath familiar—
clearly, not all messengers pour out vials

of destruction or braid glass chips into a saint's
leather belt. Some must be sent to teeter
on the edge of a smoke-filled room, watching

color spatter as the wheel revolves and light
plucks the fine grooves of a guitar's steel strings.
Were they supposed to tell us something?

It's all mixed up now with the singer's breath
deep in the mike, her lowered head,
hair falling over a half-whispered rasp,

collapse of ice cubes in an untouched glass,
a match scrape's millisecond of nothing,
and then—the blue birth of flame.

HERE

Wharves with their warehouses sagging
  on wooden slats, windows steamed up
    and beaded with rain—it's a wonder

weather doesn't wash them away. In time,
  they seem to say, you'll be gone too,
    your belongings left on a quay for the taking . . .

What's there to do, but stroll over cobbled streets,
  listing letters you owe, books, food, anything solid—
    cement stairs, bike chains, manhole covers—

anything to give yourself weight. But later,
  sleeping, you'll run like rain downhill
    back to those ramshackle buildings

stacked like crates, windows pitted with salt,
  doors barely held by their hinges.
    You'll be there, on the slotted dock

with its barnacled pilings, its green
  weedy skirts that shimmy in slow time
    against wave wrack and slump: at home

in that floating world, as water unravels
  masts into rippling flags. You'll hear
    engine grind, halyard clank, and fog's

ghostly horn declaring water takes all
   in the end. Or is that the voice of some other
     shadowy self just wanting to see

how insubstantial we are, how loosely moored
   to everything solid—and yet, here,
     for a time, within this wash of oilslick

and cloud drift, this long-stemmed sea,
   star-floating, gull-feathered, where all things
     that have to end, begin.

BACKWASH

Bad times, and I go back in my mind
  to the rail of the drawbridge spanning
    Barnegat Bay, the distant sails
flaring in wind, mackerel sky,
  whitecaps above, below. And play
    this back one more time: the boy
who gassed up yachts at the boat basin,
  how he'd saunter into the snack bar,
    karate chop the jukebox and watch
that disk gently clatter down. *Louie,*
  Louie. Cut to my sister, the waitress,
    covering her ears, yelling, "Get out,"
while he stares from behind one greased
  dangling curl, refusing to budge.
    Sullen look, positively poured into those jeans.
Who says there's just one safe way to walk,
  one road properly lit, and the rest—
    all slippery water, unmarked? Who knows
what I was doing up there
  on the bridge's slow rise, the concrete
    rail's scuffed glitter, wind's sweet
bantering torque? Ask my sister why
  she ran out screaming, tugged so hard
    I had to roll her way, or plunge
to the stone embankment the tide bared.
  She shoved me at a chair, dialed Mother,
    but I didn't hear what she said, I just

stared so hard I *was* that boy
  gunning engines straight toward the slip,
    so hard he's still inside me now,
slamming them into reverse just as the yachts
  would have splintered against the dock.
    No expression on his pocked face,
everything he felt poured into throttle and gas.
  Boat, backwash, bridge, channel cut
    deep as thought no flashlight can pierce.
And underneath? Who says it's all jellyfish,
  tar, sharks, storm tide ripping things
    out to sea? Ah, *Louie, Louie,* there are times
I go back to those whitecaps ruffling the sky,
  that light streaking the steel-colored bay below.
    No money, bad dreams, and the moon
come so close I can see the worry written
  all over its face, big shock of some new loss
    up ahead. I need a little edge, a glare,
that first splintering sound of dock
  starting to give. Play it back one more time:
    sputtering gas-smell, sunlit backwash
swamping boat, piling, pier—all of which,
  in that one fine moment unlike most, the boy
    utterly owned, and the boy gave to me.

BASS LINE

FOR MILT HINTON

He needs a bigger body, bull fiddle
to make that thump, that deeper pulse, he needs

four fat inflexible strings made of gut
wrapped by steel, so he can pluck each night

that tree and its strange fruit, its slumped shoulders,
and bulging eyes. . . . As he fingers the neck,

as he frets, keeps the time, he can take
those naked feet hung like weights on a stopped clock.

If it's too much to say one sight winds up
a life and keeps it running, still

some things are burned into the eyes
like a maker's mark seared into walnut

belly or back, history always there,
no matter how the body is patched

and reglued, the gut and steel fine-tuned.
It's a deep groove in the brain,

whether you play on top or behind the beat,
walk the line or break out: to know a man

can be waiting for a train and because the crowd's
riled up get taken. If death unmakes him,

maybe music's a way of weeping,
of cradling the broken body,

its strained neck, its eyes that tried to jump
at what they saw, and sad hands, sad hands

that couldn't lift to brush a fly.
Night after night, rhythm wants to unwind

the wire cable from that tree, sway
the mob away from its drunken rush.

So if he humps that stiff body night
after night, if he slaps and slaps? It's to

accent the offbeat, strengthen the weak, swing
like somebody who knows what swinging is.

TRANSITION

Beside this pond a mockingbird perched
on the top branch of a waxy magnolia
begins her song: three simple notes,

then a complicated run, then she squawks
like a crow—back and forth, notes and braided trill,
something else I can't grasp, punctuated

with that crow blat, as if she's pushing
a sax so far out she has to flutter back,
start over, from the top, voice after voice,

squeeze horn, clank and drum, a regular
one-person band—not unlike that actor
who came to my high school, one man playing

all the parts in *Macbeth*. He'd turn his back, pass
a hand over his face, and spool from witch to general
to Lady egging him on. Scary as hell,

all those voices pooled inside.
And the way he'd recompose himself—
like Coltrane in *Transition*, transforming

solace to scream and back, each voice reaching,
he says in the liner notes, not toward
someone else's throne, but his own

always shifting "better self." I'd love to believe
it's easy for birds: they just open their throats
and music spills, trill after trill, three

clear notes, then—to keep it cool—a little Coltrane,
but without the strain, without that ache
for a note just out of reach, or so deep inside

it shatters when it hits the air. Maybe
a bird *is* all instinct and moment, no ambition,
no *better* and *worse* driving it to the edge of song.

But as Lady Macbeth, her world crashing,
that actor was so haggard and bent,
I was terrified of him, or her,

or myself feeling his voices stir the voices in me,
the way a fish leaping stirs the pond, makes depth
suddenly real, and something like death,

that little death we die each time we see
we're blind to what's below. Listening hard now,
I know when the bird finishes her set

she'll fly off—as if half the tune
is always somewhere else, beyond,
completing and undoing us at once.

BOOK OF NUMBERS

1
Before we wrote on sheep skins with blood,
before we chiseled on rocks the number
of war dead and missing, before we learned

to count by company and platoon,
didn't we heap small stones, counting *one*
and *one* and *one* as sheep ambled past?

Before we learned to divide, was the present
fluid, did future and past circle around us
like stars, like luminous moons rising,

the light rain of seeds falling from a hand?
Or so a child might wonder, dangling
upside down on the couch, blood rushing

to her head, feet in the air, as she dreams
of the ceiling's spackled room, all the old
furniture gone, so anything might happen.

2

Out of the chemical bath a young man sharpens
into focus. The concentration of his gaze,

the large bread crumb in his hand bidding
the creature come, and the pigeon in mid-air,

its wings fanning the light, are one clear moment
my daughter pins to the wall. Print after print

she raises him—now in the stylized gesture
of a saint, one bird on his finger, one treading air,

now many birds, their wings blurred
as if no shutter's faster than time.

Then a last image drips from her hand:
the spackled sidewalk, one crumb like a hub

around which fat pigeons cluster
with inscrutable writings on their wings,

with rounded heads facing in like spokes,
and many eyes about to meet and spark

a mystical wheel that could lift up
from my daughter's hand, rising

with a sound like many waters, a sound
like thunder, like tumult whirring up, wheel

within wheel, rising toward brightness, a voice
within the flame, a message in the voice,

a burning in that message for the one
who may not know what it says, but stops

to listen and see—everywhere the seed,
the spark, the wing, trembling fire.

3

Our young son would run up and down the long
hallway, untied shoelaces askitter, making up
rules for death. The photo of my father as a boy
in a high chair holding an ivory elephant—
he couldn't be dead. Just old men die, right?

Not little boys. Only very bad boys who run out
in front of cars after their mothers said no, right?
What does he think now, this young man
in green scrubs, a little bleary eyed as the night's
crises are brought in: the stabbed, the stroked-out,

the shot, the one with feathers stuck in his hair,
and homemade stigmata, saying he is
the true prophet of God, and thus stepped
boldly into the glint of oncoming cars.
Only bad people with guns, right? Say it, say it.

Now he knows more than I do about the night
and its wounds, the dry bones, the trembling
frame. My son—who once when I answered
in exasperation, I don't know,
said, You do, you have to—now leans over

a grimacing body, asks where does it hurt,
when did it start, puts on rubber gloves and touches
the pain—here? here?—working against time,
not counting higher than one, each wounded,
obstreperous, pulsing and fragile soul.

4

Is this the only comfort allowed, just this—
that after everyone has died who will die
in one terrible year, you may find yourself

outside the hospital, leaning against a young tree,
gazing into the leafy light of its branches?
If past and future are one continuous stirring

of light through air, if counting begins with *one*
and in the eyes of God never moves on,
if prayer begins with touch and ends in vision

whirring up like birds wheeling at the edge
of sight, if the dead aren't just bands of light,
or layers of loam, and their voices haven't slipped

so far out they've become inaudible waves
in ever-thinning densities of space, if something
of them still lingers, they might sound in this tree

like the veery whose fluid downward spiral
of sound you've never heard before,
its eerie flute making the air tremble.

THE BIRD SUIT

I was thinking of a bird suit. Not Big Bird,
or a Vegas can-can number with sequins,
but more like the ones in the movie
I'd been ditching classes to watch all week,
mostly just me in the empty theater.

Still shots of dying Indians,
the camera like the last stage, after
forced marches and disease, everyone
nostalgic now that it's over, ending
with turn-of-the century footage:

a gray flickering Pacific Northwest,
longboats lurching toward shore, dancers
in the prow turning great beaked heads
side to side, their enormous wings
flushing the inside out. Each afternoon

I'd step from that world into the fading light,
not thinking about dissertations,
just frayed quills and split seams, masks
smelling of seaweed, pine pitch, old breath.
I wanted ratty wings strapped with cracked leather

heavy as barbells to budge. Hawk, harpy—
to be anything but little sparrow
pecking her dutiful crumbs. All week
I watched those birds come closer,
beating their cumbersome wings—fierce

totem beaks, knees bent for ballast,
boats pitching across the bay
as rowers gouge the choppy seas.
Drums pulsing faster and faster,
potlatch host on shore watching them loom.

Then he's giving away blankets and bowls,
down to bare walls, and was I crazy
to be handing back my fellowship—
half-running down the hall, heading out
to the last matinee, to see one more time

what comes after those boats
scrape through pebbles, reenter the hiss
and spray of waves? The host alone now,
cleaned out, empty-handed, nothing
he owns left to own him, no letters

after his name. The birds making off
with his bright future, and nothing
to turn him from those wings disappearing
into the gray, uncrushable surf,
its grainy flickering black and white.

The Life of Keats, Spared Briefly by John Coltrane

When *The Life of Keats* is just too much
 I look at the postcard keeping my place:
  Claxton photo, Newport, 1960,
Coltrane on makeshift stairs, climbing
 to the stage. Everything's on the rise,
  even the tenor in his hand
parallels the railing's upward slant. Clear day,
 sharp contrasts—what luck to capture
  his dark suit against the plywood siding's
bright grain. What good eyes to see
 this moment ascending, itself a solo
  amped by light, image snapped fast
as the riffs Coltrane's about to play.
 And Keats—wouldn't he have loved
  passing a bottle of claret among friends
on the Newport lawn, shading his eyes
 in afternoon light, nodding perhaps
  as if he could see the notes scatter,
then reflock, small birds gathering in trees,
 or coasting above the stage, and in his mind
  a new ode beginning to form . . .
Would it contain these long fingers
 around the horn, the battered speakers,
  the grain's turbulent swirls? Would he be torn

between stopping time right here
  on the sunlit stairs, or letting it flow,
    chord into chord, toward some note just out
of reach—a sound always on the verge,
  half heard, then gone? "But look,"
    the photo seems to say, "isn't it all
right here—Coltrane's contained adrenaline,
  his knit brows, eyes in shadow
    as if turned inward to concentrate
this moment into muse? Vivid sax,
  bright rail, foot rising to the next step—
    this is beauty, *this* is truth."
And yet in my book it's all over for Keats,
  nothing left but the slow anguished dissolve,
    the fountain outside, water rising,
then falling back into dissolution.
  What can the photo say to that—
    "I saw a man gathering intensity,
and could not stop his passing"?
  I stood on the sidewalk watching
    my daughter drive off to college alone
for the first time, not knowing the card
  was tucked in a book waiting to be sent.
    "I found this," she wrote, "and thought
you'd love it," which I do, love being
  held here, before the next step, in the gap
    between songs, half hearing the first bars
of the next, as if whole lives can be
  rewound, reread, lives that I know
    are gone—like music as it passes through us
and keeps on moving, in waves or light,
  till only those without ears can hear it.

EXCHANGE

My dog was barking at rocks, but where was
our neighborhood school, its parking lot,
the broken fence by the shut-down warehouse?
All I could see was the VA hospital,
the psych floor on top, and a man at the window.
Like that stifling before a swoon,
around me the air was hot. Suddenly
I was a candle wick trying to keep
from getting snuffed—not by men
or women or passing toughs. They
would have saved me.
                              Maybe I flickered
in the jittery eye of that wrecked vet.
Me, in my peacenik flannel shirt,
my feminist pants and stammerer's shoes—
scuffed, thick-tongued, double-knotted—
I was talking to myself, trying to name
this strange feeling, to explain, explain:
me and my smart-girl glasses, my watch,
the world spinning and my skin's countless
invisible antennae flushed and stinging.
I sank my face into the dog's blond fur,
and with each lap of her tongue got licked down
to something very small, a seed.
                              A bird
could have swallowed me, or a man
at a window watching late sun flare

the glass, dreading night coming down,
and the land-mined dark. What did I step on,
to be hurled through the wrong end
of a telescope, squeezed by someone's squint,
so small my face didn't matter,
the shape of my lips and eyes? Still,
I threw the rock for my dog to bring back,
wet, held softly in her mouth. *Skittering
Flame*, I thought, *Fluttering Sparrow,
Flickering Soul*—
                        as if I had stumbled
into the mind of someone trying
to finish a war. As if it was for more than
ourselves we tossed and retrieved, lost
and found that rock—look—still unexploded.
For more than herself my dog sniffed and rolled,
jumped up unharmed, and I lost everything
I thought I knew. If so, then it was
for more than himself that the man stood
at his burning window, shaky but
holding on, his hands cupped to the hot glass,
determined to see us through.

To Walt Whitman in Heaven

Things that look good and aren't: high fashion,
Manifest Destiny, limp wires the electrician thinks
are dead till he grabs hold and then, O Infinite-
coursing-through-finite—thank God his spastic dance

is only a shock—one yelp and he shakes
it off. Not so easy for the girl next door
feeling her first kiss begin to fester
as the young man's buddies drive by hooting

and one calls out, *how far did ya get? Whadda
we owe?* It's enough to make everything
look bad. So, a list then of what turns out
to be good: the loud-mouthed parrot

down the block that scared off two robbers,
the junior prom I spent alone in my room
reading you, Walt Whitman, your great
barbaric yawp entering my mind like salt

water coursing through fresh, stinging my wounds,
till every image was sharp—the lunatic,
the lily-faced boy in the makeshift hospital,
contralto, runaway, cloud scud, your voice

whispering through sea spray to ferry crowds,
just as you feel, so I felt. . . . What doesn't change
and remain, remain and grow strange? The lace
bodice from my mother's slip my daughter

now sews onto the cuffs of her new jeans,
the crooked front tooth that has traveled through
how many kisses from my mother's mouth
to mine, and on to my son. What is a list?

The neighbor girl goes through her catalog
of moves under the hoop—sky hooks, lay-ups,
fall-away jumpers. Long after dark, she's out there
dribbling her heart on the asphalt, tossing it up,

nothing but net. Painful, yes, but how else
will she get to that sweet agony within,
your great loitering contradictions? She dodges
and spins, as if shedding a skin, steps around

the driveway to keep the motion light flaring
as she passes from shadow into Technicolor,
banks a shot, jabs the air to cheer herself on,
point guard, center and crowd all in one,

and I almost see you in the dark,
on the fringe, though I can hardly say what
you mean, in the sweet mysterious night vapor
hovering over blacktop and lamp-green lawn.

READING

Because the titmice at the feeder are
all silk and tufted gray, and the cardinals
beautifully paired in their marriage
of subtle and brash, I have to read
the same sentence seven times,
then finally give up and study instead
the suggestions of bright red flashing
as house finches occupy the feeder.
On my lap an essay explaining
Dickinson's deft ironies, elusive
dashes and slants, so dense I have to stop
wanting to get to the end, the bottom
of anything, and just live in the drift
of phrase and clause, until once again
a feathered thing—a nuthatch heading down
a rutted trunk—catches my eye, and I
am torn like an old uneasy treaty,
within a single mind two tribes dwelling,
people of the book, yes, but also others
literate in seed husk, rain slant, cloud.

IMPEDIMENTS

After all those years of throat lock and panic
at the lips, roadblock, detour, paratroopers
balking—what if you just said, *Yes* now, softly,
or shouted *Amen*, agreeing with the preacher

like the Hammond B3 that answers him,
phrase for phrase? No more stammer and ruse,
quick switch to a safer word, slippery mind
faster than the mouth, so the world's all translation.

Think of dreams and their fluid dynamics,
how craziest things make sense, consonants
connect, tongue twisters of impossible
events flow like rivers. In one you rose

on foam, up through the narrow neck
of a Coke bottle, emerging to applause
in a mink coat, then let it drop and stepped
into a galvanized tub. Was it meaning

you carried all these years, or that flattened
then fluffed out fur, the ribbed bottle's
pale enclosure opening to sun glint
on stippled gray—each detail a variation

on getting "saved," though that word's too simple.
It needs unpronounceable roots, syllables
that don't quite mesh, raising questions
of usage and stress, old coats to be shed,

resentments dropped, enemies coaxed out
and coddled, and—ah, the enemy within,
that stymied child unable to say a word
without foot stomps and blinks, unable to let

a thought come easy and smooth. So much
feeling coiled inside her, a mouthful of sparks,
and everything outside combustible—
one *amen* away from bursting into flame.

Sister

She slumps down on the curb and trails her hand
through rain spill, the street's loose neon
flickering toward the gutter—a young woman,
but she looks more like a child now, hunched up

in the back seat watching a road dissolve
into ribbons. Hard to believe that minutes ago
in the bookstore she slurred, *you tell 'em, Honey,*
as a poet read, then stumbled forward,

shaking her head, saying *Wha? wha?*
I don't unnerstan, grabbing a chair back,
missing, till just before the podium
a man swung her around and shoved her out.

Remember those dreamy thoughts, little hums,
and letting your eyes blur so where you've been
just unravels? I can't count all the nights
Mother drove, while my sister replayed

a recital she thought she botched. But once,
our car stopped for gas, and there by the curb,
a tree blazed up, spotlit and lizard green
with a spangly sheen I've only seen

since in old movies—say, a washed-up
lounge singer leaning into the mike,
flushed by the late hour and light. My sister
was weeping by then that she'd never be

good enough, huge sobs caught in her throat,
and the tree was swaying, each leaf
a sequin sewn on the slinky dress,
catching and tossing out light. In that movie

the diva's beat, her tone burnt and smoky,
but still she fills the screen, so even now
through rain, through chartreuse neon pouring
into storm drains, she could say to a lush,

that's all right, Honey, I don't unnerstan
either, her song dedicated to the one
starting to slip, who's loosened her grip,
the one who needs that rough blended voice,

which even crushed, even sucking up car fumes,
still calls us by name—me, and my sister,
and this young drunk—each of us the same
sweet and throaty, viscous, translucent *Honey.*

STRAY HORN

Three blocks into my run, I'm too stubborn
to turn back, though the Walkman's batteries
are shot, so James Carter's "A Train"
slows to a garbled bloat of sound,
a syrupy ooze backed up, clogging
the saxophone's tubes. Smell of exhaust,
a bad muffler in this song, clank
of something wrong, tailpipe dragging
its metallic rasp. And we're running
out of gas, me and this sax, elongated
screech of brakes aching toward resolution,
one note going on and on till it's got
to burst, become the rumble and flap
of driving on a flat, scattering

roadside cinders and trash—but scratch that.
This guy is good. Even on the tape's
last gasp, his breath blows past road blocks,
swerves around hairpin turns, valves knocking,
gravity his guide, arriving at
such a viscous tone, it's as if he played
through viscera, deep throat of God
straying from those seven trumpets of doom
to commandeer this horn, its music
of muscle and bone, magnetic pull
of breath swirling through the tape's
winded spin, through my sore shins,

spent lungs, run done, walking the last block
stunned by the belly, the being of song.

GOSPEL HOUR

The good news is how happy she looks,
this daughter who struggled to bloom—
for so many years, more like a bulb

planted upside down, fist sunk
in the ground. But she's thriving now,
bursting with sobriety's slogans,

adding her voice in little riffs
to the gospel song blasting
over the shower, its lyrics dissolving

into *Yes*, just, *Yesss*, that pure assent.
And if I could sing, mostly I'd agree,
though I'd have made the world without

disease and mosquitoes, without
country music, bread mold, warring sects,
Disney, those teen years when you'd

eat window glass just to get the hell out.
Of course, there'd be no need, then,
for this singer to lift her voice

to such a height as the shower stops,
the *Gospel Hour* swells to a chorus of wails,
the whole choir joining in, *Yes, Oh yesss*.

Meanwhile, downstairs, the cat
tips over the garbage, and the tulips,
bending with the weight of their purple cups,

won't stop unfolding, even though
it will mean their demise, their petals
so far open—I can't explain,

but maybe my daughter could,
or the singer behind the bathroom door,
who is taking just one note, and petal

by petal, *love me, love me not,* pulling
out an entire scale. Then she's edging
herself to a last gravelly high pitch,

backed up by my daughter's throaty hums,
while the choir's at ease, having finished
its moaning and wails, so if a door

opened right now, we'd see through the mist
dozens of unstrained faces, exposed
and gleaming, like flowers spread so wide

just the pistil and stamen remain,
little nerves, antennae—as if that's where
the music meant to take us all along.

Meditation, with Other Voices

Lake Huron

Damp September morning. Gray sky, the texture
of dense feathers, mist on the verge of rain,

the breakwater jutting far into gray-green fog—
even if all this fades, to have been here,

to have written *the slash of waves on shore*,
misspelling *shore* in a quick hand, *sure* . . .

To have wakened early, far from home,
churning through your mind thoughts of work,

unfinished, flawed. And while the other
wedding guests sleep in cabins along the shore

(weed scent, sound of stones rattled by waves),
to have put on shoes, gone running beside whitecaps

flaring through fog, then uphill toward town,
damp air sculpting around your body

everything it knows, and everything it doesn't.
To find in the small park a drinking fountain

shaped like a lion's mouth, its faucet deep inside,
so you think twice about putting your head

into those concrete jaws. Then (out of where?)
you hear a voice say, *Fear Not*. Your own mind

like a flute another plays? Or memory's chorus
reciting, *You are anxious about many things;*

only one is needful. . . . (What, what?)
And whose voice now, across how many tens

or hundreds of years, saying, *To love this world
is to love fate?* The *shape* of fate rising

and falling in waves? The *maker* of fate?
Fait, you write by mistake—*fait accompli,*

as if things are ever finished, not just caught up
in a greater motion. . . . Now, these wild and raw waves

crashing the breakwater, the lighthouse horn
picking up the question. *What matters?*

To have been here, simply? To see gray mist,
slate sea, slash of waves, chicory, ironweed,

coreopsis, this small Midwestern town built on mills,
smokestacks, breakwaters, ore ships against the horizon,

profit, profiteering—always that hard labor.
But (the bride and groom are radiant) love, too,

and the ever-present foghorn telling us how blind
we are, how much more there is. So, what to do,

but put your head in the lion's mouth and drink?
Your dark past—those words form, whatever they mean—

whatever is lost, distant, frightening, capable
of turning radiant, spraying up, swamping the jetty?

LATE PSALM

I am hating myself for the last time.
  I'm rolling up angst like a slice of bread,
squishing it into a glob that will rot
  into blue medicine—another joke,
delivered by God, who when you finally
  elbow and nudge to the front of the line,
says, *Oh, but the first shall be last. . . .*
  I'm considering the roadside grass,
all dressed up and headed straight for the fire.
  "Who isn't?" say the flames,
though it's easy to pretend not to hear
  in this mountain resort with its windows
all finely dressed for the busiest season
  filled with glass fish, turquoise earrings,
infusers that turn weeds into tea.
  "Who isn't poor already?" sing the stalks
of dried milkweed, though it's hard to
  imagine these shoppers in bright ski jackets
coated with road grit, dust from the chunks
  of bituminous coal left outside mines
for the poor to glean. The poor—
  just driving by those bent figures,
filling their plastic bags, here in the 1990s,
  made me stop nodding *yeah yeah*
to the music and pull off the road,
  stunned by the way the years press hard

to fossilize plants, and the poor too,
  who seem to age a month for every
middle-class day. How could they
  possibly hear a blade of grass sigh, "Poor?
There is no such thing." Did I say
  I'm hating myself for the last time?
It's not easy, but I'm loving instead—
  brown teeth, Kool Aid mustaches, swollen
knuckles, nature's answer to all questions—
  prodigality, those countless insects
and missionary weeds spending themselves
  freely and as far as I can tell, never
rescinding a thing. I'm loving a man
  with his pockets full of pen caps, receipts,
crumpled dollars to put in a beggar's
  dented cup, briefcase bulging with papers,
leftover crusts for the ducks,
  and out of his eyes little fish of light,
glimmering minnows and fingerlings
  leaping between us, flashing
like the tiny carp we watched last night
  in the restaurant tank, appearing through
weeds, miniature castles, a bubbly
  tube resuscitating their atmosphere.
Do they ever conceive of worlds outside
  the only one they've known? Because *he* is,
my man says they're serene, swimming in
  a seamless rippling universe,
not quaking at the sight of monstrous eyes
  leering into the tank, not aching
with the lure of light, lethal burn of air,
  declaring their world a glass prison house.
Rich or poor—who decides? Who wrote
  the stories in which women cry out

all the more when folks tell them to hush,
  and beggars asking for money
get wild rapture instead?

BECAUSE WE IMAGINE A JOURNEY

and don't know how difficult the passage,
we leave gifts to help the dead cross over:
my teacher's black beret tucked in her coffin,

my nephew's notebooks, in case he needs
to recall how long he resisted the demons.
And for the small child freshly buried,

each time I walk the dog there's something new—
another pinwheel, a stuffed rabbit,
ceramic angel, photo of her mother

wrapped in plastic and tape—
as if someone whispered, Fly, *little soul,*
back here, and hover. All summer

that someone was pleading,
the way I see now I must have been,
in September, making the minister open

cupboards and desks for something to hold
a few granules of my mother.
But when he poured the rest of her out

in the churchyard, under a cross made of shrubs,
with the family gathered, it seemed wrong
to hold anything back from the journey,

even a part so small it fit
in a brown plastic medicine bottle.
No wonder the bagpiper practices here

his eerie songs—so unearthly they could be
wails made by souls force-marched off,
and loath to go, bunched up

like crowds at a border, great ghostly hordes
that pick up the song when the piper stops,
gusts driving a throng of leaves skittering

up the steep road. Such a huge wind
it surges through trees, bends them nearly in two,
and as if to linger in the tumult longer

an elderly couple walks backward
uphill, hand-in-hand, as I head down
pulled by my dog who stops to sniff the air,

then shakes his tags, lunging happily
toward the cattails and feathered water
of the pond. Watching ducks skid in,

materializing from all directions,
raucous and comic, around a man's
magnetic bag of crumbs, I can't help thinking

it's possible there is no death after all,
just a thin veil between one life and another,
lifting sometimes in a wail, or wind, an eddy

of leaves wrapping itself around the legs
of a grieving mother, or telling a child
it's all right, all right now, to let go.

LAST BOAT

We were waiting for the ferry,
lolling on the lowest ramp, on floats,
shitty with wave slush, dip and sway.

We were sun-seared, sapped, soaking in
the latticework, wooden scaffolding,
stacks of lobster traps, pilings stained black

from creosote and tar, green with seaweed
combed out on receding waves, swirled back
by water's slap and curl: levels and lengths

of working docks, creaky planks, crossbars
of tacked asbestos for stopping the slip
on slick days—the whole wet rush,

the gleaming run-down fertile place.
We were sitting on a dock of the bay,
watching how matter melts into

quivery silks of light, a brilliant seethe,
a glittery tease of *there*
and *not there*, such dazzling manna.

We were squinting through shadows
at little flamelike fish flickering
among weeds—a whole world it seemed

flaring under the ramshackle,
barnacled, rock-bottom dock, all flow
and flown, and we were resting in

the brevity, the breve, breviary,
the never-ending not-me: waiting
for the ferry, wishing it wouldn't come.

At the Public Market (*III*)

Pineapples all patchwork and spikes,
with green rooster crowns; pomegranates
catacombed, and in each small waxy room

an edible jewel; barrels
of lumpen potatoes, country onions
and their city cousins, the lilies,

decked out in fancy names like handles
to grasp when the petals are gone: *Adelina*,
Latoya, Louvre, Solomio . . .

And tiny peppers with no earthly use
but to be viewed; coffee beans burlapped
and brought from Kenya, Zimbabwe, Peru;

wheels and wedges of cheese, balls and bricks,
made with mold, the whey whipped out,
so the curds can curdle, be coated

with linen, bark, grape leaves or wax, then left
to sit and age like old folks in rockers—
we eat what time does to earth, fragrant

or foul. Even when Dante gets to heaven
and there's no more plot, just shadowless light,
saints content with their allotted flames,

even there, he meets a widow with more lovers
than she can name, blazing among the rest,
happily spared for her generous heart.

And maybe our best chance, yet, is to believe
the world's not empty, not *nothing* in fine clothes,
but *everything*, marrow, muscle, skin.

The University of Wisconsin Press
Poetry Series

The Low End of Higher Things
David Clewell

Show and Tell: New and Selected Poems
Jim Daniels

Late Psalm
Betsy Sholl

Reactor
Judith Vollmer